STOP MANAGING START INSPIRING

Keys for Leaders
To Bring Out the
Best In Others

J. L. ASHMORE

Edited by Kathy Sparrow, San Diego, CA www.kathysparrow.com

Formatting and cover design by Dawn Teagarden, Teagarden Designs, Las Vegas, Nevada www.TeagardenDesigns.com

Printed in the United States.

ISBN: 978-0-615-81278-6

Disclaimer: The purpose of this book is to educate. This publication is designed to give accurate and authoritative information with regard to the subject matter covered. If professional, legal, or therapeutic advice or other expert assistance is required, the service of a competent professional should be sought. The author does not guarantee that anyone following the tips, ideas, suggestions, techniques, or strategies will become successful.

For more information on leadership and other topics offered by the author, go to:
www.stopmanagingstartinspiring.com

Contact the author at
info@stopmanagingstartinspiring.com

About the Author

Author, J. L. (Jani) Ashmore has over 30 years of experience as a leader, speaking and consulting in the corporate world. As well, she has worked in organizations offering programs on personal development and spirituality. She has been an Amazon.com bestselling author, international speaker, and consultant affecting the success of hundreds of organizations and thousands of individuals in technology, telecommunications, government, financial, utilities, and a variety of other industries.

She has contributed to such organizations as: Bank of America, Charles Schwab, Kaiser Permanente, Motorola, Rockwell Automation, Air Canada, Federal Express, USDA, City of Seattle, HP, Sabre Computer Systems, British Telecom, and others.

Jani has facilitated workshops and consulting interventions to Fortune 500 corporations in the U.S. as well as Canada, Europe, and Asia Pacific. She has served personnel ranging from executives to front-line employees in such areas as Leadership, Empowerment, Sales, Communication Skills, Customer Service, Valuing Diversity, Team Building, and Train-the-Trainer.

Jani has been a contributing author to two Amazon.com bestsellers. One is a business oriented book called *Nothing But Net* and the other is about finding success in all areas of your life, called *Success Secrets*.

She has trained with America's #1 Success Coach, Jack Canfield, co-creator of the *Chicken Soup for the Soul* series and author of the best-selling book, *The Success Principles*. Working with the Canfield Training Group, Jani has been part of the delivery team training students in the success principles and is featured in Jack's acclaimed instructional videos *Success Profiles* along with John Gray author of *Men are From Mars Women are from Venus*, Lisa Nichols, Motivational Speaker/Author, and Timothy Ferris author of *The 4 Hour Work Week* as well as other thought leaders.

Jani has had a keen interest in the behavioral sciences and human potential throughout her adult life. In addition to other specific technologies, Jani has studied and practiced Neuro-Linguistic Programming (NLP). She has been a trainer in the human potential movement for Tony Robbins and facilitates *"the work"* by Byron Katie. She also coaches individuals to live a balanced yet inspiring life. As a test of her own human potential, she has accomplished a black belt in Karate, completed the San Francisco marathon, has proven herself as a firewalker, and has hiked the Grand Canyon from rim to rim. Her commitment to her own personal development is an inspiration unto itself.

With a unique combination of experience plus an enthusiasm for providing quality service, Jani's clients have said her contributions to them and their organizations have been notable.

Jani resides in southern California.

Other Works by J. L. Ashmore

Amazon.com Best Sellers:

Success Secrets
Co-authored with Jack Canfield and others.

Jack Canfield, America's #1 Success Coach and co-creator of the legendary *Chicken Soup for the Soul*™ best-selling book series, brought together today's foremost thought leaders to reveal for the first time in print their own incredible success secrets. It includes inspiration and motivation to move forward — as well as the proven action steps that attract abundance and bring fulfillment. These innovative experts deliver all that and more — because they have the spirit and skills to transform your life and help you create the wealth, health, and happiness you've been waiting for.

Nothing But Net
Co-authored with James Malinchak and others.

Some of the world's leading speakers, trainers, and entrepreneurs reveal their life-changing secrets that empower individuals and organizations to profit when times are tough and triumph over challenges that seem insurmountable. These are the experts who have built their careers on enabling their clients to become healthier, wealthier, and wiser. Benefit from their years of experience as well as their breakthrough ideas that have transformed organizations, teams and individual lives. Rise up from the negative and embrace the best tomorrow you can imagine. Enjoy *Nothing But Net* for years to come!

Video/DVD Series

Success Profiles

This DVD series features note-worthy authors, speakers and thought leaders such as:

J. L. Ashmore, *Stop Managing/Start Inspiring: Keys for Leaders to Bring Out the Best in Others*

Timothy Ferriss, Author, *The 4-Hour Work Week*

Jack Canfield, New York Times Best Selling Author, *The Success Principles*

James Malinchak, Author/Speaker, Featured on ABC TV''s Secret Millionaire

John Gray, New York Times Best Selling Author, *Men Are From Mars, Women Are From Venus*

Lisa Nichols, Author/Speaker, *No Matter What*

Jim Bunch, Founder of *The Ultimate Game of Life*

Joe Sweeney, New York Times Best Selling Author, *Networking is a Contact Sport*

Ivan Misner, Founder of Business Network International

Marcia Wieder, Author/Speaker, *Making Your Dreams Come True*

Alison Armstrong, Author, *Keys to the Kingdom*

Les Hewitt, Author, *The Power of Focus: How to Hit Your Business, Personal and Financial Targets with Absolute Certainty*

To order any of the above or to book J. L. Ashmore as a speaker for your event or as a consultant in your organization, email:
info@stopmanagingstartinspiring.com

Or go to:
www.stopmanagingstartinspiring.com
www.JLAshmore.com

This book is dedicated to my parents, George and Margie Ashmore, for their inspiration and belief in me. They were models of leadership and living life to its fullest. I am grateful for all the love, guidance, and encouragement they gave me as I was growing up and as an adult.

Acknowledgments

I have been so fortunate to work with a variety of leaders and teachers throughout my life. They have inspired me, mentored and coached me, sometimes kicked me in the behind to keep me moving, but have always shown their heart and desire to pass on the ripple effect of making a difference in my life and onto the lives of others I encounter. I am grateful for all of them.

I applaud my editor, Kathy Sparrow and designer, Dawn Teagarden for their expertise, creativity, patience, and TLC. You both treated me and my work with respect, care and support through one of the more tedious aspects of the publishing process. You're the best!

A special thank you goes to Patty Aubrey, President of Canfield Training Group and author of multiple books from the *Chicken Soup for the Soul* series. She acted as a midwife as I gave birth to this book. Her mentoring and belief in me will be forever appreciated. She is one of the most inspiring and motivating leaders in my life.

Thank you to the many family and friends for the support in seeing this project to completion. I am especially grateful to my family — daughter, Tamara; son-in-law, Marc, and granddaughters, Laurel and Calli — who make my life so rich and full of all that makes life worth living. I love you all from the bottom of my heart!

Foreword

Although I was raised on a dairy farm in Colorado, my parents were leaders in our community in the rural organizations in which we were members. They gave me the gift of that model and encouraged me and all my siblings to step out, be and do the best we could, and live a full life. I believe their model of leadership is a legacy that lives on in me to be shared with others.

Throughout my life, I have consistently stepped out to be a leader in many of the groups and organizations in which I have been involved. I have spent decades developing myself personally and professionally. I have had a unique desire to test my human potential and to continue expanding to my fullest potential. I believed Helen Keller when she said, *"Life is either a daring adventure or nothing."*

In that vein, I have found myself do such things as becoming a black belt in karate, running marathons, parachuting and tandem sky diving out of airplanes, walking on hot burning coals, and the most difficult one for people to believe bending rebar at my neck. These goals and actions may sound crazy, but each time I achieved such a goal, it became a reference for me to ask, "If I didn't think I could do that and I did, what else in life could I possibly do?"

I don't suggest you have to do such things to be a better leader. I do believe, however, that it is important for leaders to be a model of moving through challenges and limiting beliefs whether they are ones found in the workplace or ones demonstrated in their personal lives.

The workplace today is filled with challenges and obstacles to getting the job done. Some managers and leaders are effective at clearing those challenges and obstacles. Many employees would say that their managers or the leaders of the organization *are* the challenge or obstacle to getting the job done. Are you a leader that inspires those you lead or might those you lead say you are part of the problem?

This book looks at roles of the leader that help you to be the kind of leader others find inspiring and want to emulate and follow. It looks at the kind of leader that inspires people to be and do their best because, as a leader, you model the same for them in a way that displays your authenticity but doesn't hide your own humanity.

You will also find this book to define a leader as anyone who steps forward and models bringing out the best in themselves and others. So, if you are an individual contributor, you will find much here that will apply to you as well.

I have been showing leaders and those they lead what makes them effective in their work for several decades. In addition to leadership skills, I have taught and consulted organizations in sales, customer service, empowerment, valuing diversity, team building, managing change, and train-the-trainer programs. I have been fortunate to travel the world to over 30 countries for my corporate work, personal development, and holiday travel.

It is my purpose to show others how to live to their fullest potential and continue to expand myself with the inspiring and adventurous ways that I live my life. My wish is that you will find, rediscover, or cultivate your purpose in life, set the goals, and take the actions to manifest that purpose. May that result in making you a better leader in your teams, your organization, and spill over into your personal life as well. May that then have the ripple effect in inspiring others to do the same, and thereby make a difference in the world. Thank you for your part in making this a better world for all of us!

Table of Contents

CHAPTER 1

Aspire to Inspire

> There is a difference between leadership
> and management. Leadership is of the
> spirit, compounded of personality, vision
> and training. Its practice is an art.
> Management is a science and of the
> mind. Managers are necessary.
> Leaders are indispensable.
>
> *–Admiral Thomas H. Moorer, USN*

The root of the word inspire is "inspirito" meaning "from spirit." One definition from Webster's dictionary defines spirit as: *"the... motivating, feeling part of man, often as distinguished from the body; mind; intelligence."*

Let's look at spirit, not as a religious word, but as a word that encompasses that part of us that is not physical. So in that context, let's use the phrase "to inspire" as being the kind of leader who operates in the spirit of, for example, with the attitude of wanting themselves and those around them to be and do their best. It is an attitude that inspiring leaders value.

As you read this book, think of all the times in your life you have been inspired to do your best —— how you have inspired others to do their best and how others have inspired you to do your best. The more references and examples you can find in your life, the broader your perspective of leadership will be.

Although many of the stories throughout the book are focused on the leader who has people reporting to them in a working environment, the principles you find here can be applied to anyone who takes a leadership role. Leaders aren't just those with the words "manager, executive, or supervisor" in their title. A leader can be anyone who steps forward and demonstrates effective ways of speaking, modeling, or motivating themselves and others to be the best that they can be. Leadership can be demonstrated by something as simple as picking up a piece of trash as you walk by it on the street, or being first to volunteer in your team when an unassigned task needs to be completed.

A Leader Without the Title

Some people feel their job is mindless, low paying and dead end. They look at their work as drudgery and depressing. From the book Chicken Soup for the Soul at Work, *Kenneth L. Shipley shares his story of one company that was staffed with people feeling just this way. Then, one day a new temporary worker named Jim came to work and caught the eye of one of his co-workers, Ken.*

Ken noticed Jim was different in several ways. First of all, the company did not issue uniforms, but Jim created his own uniform with khaki pants and a nicely pressed shirt with his name, Jim, embroidered on the pocket. He was never late, worked at a steady, unhurried pace, and was friendly with everyone. He took his breaks at the scheduled time with everyone else, but didn't linger past the allotted time like many others. Jim always cleaned up after himself at lunch and returned to work on time.

Jim was the kind of employee that managers love, but the other employees didn't hold that against him as sometimes happens. Jim didn't try to impress anyone or be at the top of the heap. He didn't gossip, or complain or argue with anyone. He just did his job in a way that showed his respect for himself and satisfaction he got for doing a good job — an unusual find in a low level position. Jim was a model for others — a leader. His job may have been common, but Jim wasn't.

Jim left the company when his temporary job ended. But Ken was impacted in a way that stayed with him forever. Ken started doing his job like he was a businessman fulfilling a contract, just as Jim did.

Ken's managers noticed his new way of working and promoted him. Ken went on years later to start his own business and with hard work and luck was successful. But Ken always knew that a big part of his success was the model for leadership Jim demonstrated and the lessons Jim taught Ken. As Ken said, "Respect doesn't come from the kind of work you do, it comes from the way you do the work."

So, as you continue reading this book, think of both the leader who has people reporting to them and the leader who is the individual who steps forward in whatever group they find themselves participating to model bringing out the best in themselves and others.

Managing vs. Inspiring

What's the difference in managing and inspiring? What are some of the activities and actions you associate with managing? What are some of the activities and actions you associate with inspiring? Below are some of the ideas I hear from managers and leaders when I facilitate workshops across the globe:

Managing: *reporting, scheduling, delegating, instructing, telling, planning, hiring, firing, instructing, telling, disciplining*

Inspiring: *giving feedback, motivating, encouraging, educating, listening, modeling, mentoring, guiding, asking, empowering*

Some may see tasks that are similar on each list, however in comparing the two lists you might see those tasks under "Managing" relating to the business at hand versus those under "Inspiring" relating to the people, the human side of business. Inspiring leaders see the terms related to the human side as more empowering for their employee. Managing for many conjures up additional words and phrases such as, autocratic, dis-empowering, old-school, militant. The phrase, "Do as I say, not as I do" comes to some people's minds.

True the tasks identified above in "managing" may be a required part of your job description. There are times when giving instructions is called for as a leader. You are a teacher, educator in certain circumstances. So, it is not one versus the other when I refer to the differences in managing and inspiring, I am suggesting, but the *balance* of managing and inspiring. Stop if you are *only* focusing on the managing side of your work, and start incorporating actions that inspire, if you are not already doing so, in your style of leadership.

Although many leaders naturally demonstrate inspiring techniques, there is an opportunity in organizations and teams to create an inspiring environment that encourages each member of the group as well as the manager to feel they are moving toward a common goal; in support of one another's goals as well as the team as a whole.

If you do not have people reporting to you, but aspire to be a leader even while an individual contributor, think of the difference in how you manage your job and your life versus inspire. Do you "manage" yourself by driving yourself too hard or do you encourage and inspire yourself to do the best you can while maintaining a focus on all areas of your life? Our internal self-talk can be equated to both aspects of managing and inspiring. Think of this as you continue through the chapters of this book.

A Surprising Change

My friend, Brigid, is a life and business coach who has worked for 10 years for a small company in Southern California that offers coaching and consulting to entrepreneurs. During our visits catching up on one another's lives, I have often heard stories about her company and how poorly managed the group of 10 – 12 coaches has been over the years. The coaches felt unacknowledged, disempowered, unmotivated, and undervalued. As is often the case in companies, Brigid said that the coaches often complained among themselves about management and what wasn't working. To speak to management would blackball the coach and just make their job harder. It was quite apparent the environment in their team was not a positive one.

A new manager of the coaches was hired a year ago. The first thing this manager did was to invite each coach individually to an off-site lunch meeting. He framed it as an opportunity to get to know each person and their interests if they cared to share them — a very safe environment. Because of the safe space he created, what came out in the conversations were some of the things that weren't working in the organization and possible improvements. Given the past 10 years of poor management, the coaches were surprised and excited for the chance to express themselves. Not only did this new manager listen actively and intently to what the coaches said, he acknowledged them for their ideas, appreciated them for their work, and commended their willingness to inform him of the current situation — a surprising new change for the coaches!

As well as their weekly group meetings, the new manager has continued to have the meetings individually with the coaches each quarter creating an open-door environment. He has also put into place many of the ideas the coaches brought to him when he first started his job allowing the coaches to feel valued and empowered. When I last spoke with Brigid, she mentioned that she had just recently realized that there is no longer the complaining among the coaches about management. As her friend, I can see how much more she enjoys her work now that the new manager has created an inspiring environment that supports the individual contributors in doing their best work. Some leaders

27

are an impediment to their people getting their jobs done in the best way possible. Some know how to work in tandem with their people and at the same time uplift them to achieve their highest potential. This new manager is definitely a role model of an inspiring leader.

Being a leader is a tricky balance because it requires you to not hold yourself as better than your employees — to see yourself as equal in regard to the humanity you share with them. However, it also requires you to hold a higher perspective than the employee may have — a perspective in which you can clearly hold the vision of you and your employees as a team. It takes a unique perspective to see what's good for the whole versus the single individual perspective of what's best for me, the manager.

One other aspect while we're on the topic of humanity is not being afraid to acknowledge that we all have it — our human side. True, it is as obvious as the nose on our face, yet there seems to be a tendency among some leaders to expect themselves to be perfect and not let any of their signs of weakness show. We are all human and have both strengths and weaknesses. When we allow our humanity to be acknowledged and not try to hide it, we become more authentic and approachable as leaders.

Once you have made your selection of who's the best person for the job, you communicate clearly the duties of the job, train the person to do those duties, and then empower them to do the job to the best of their ability. No one likes working under the thumb of a manager. To be empowered to make decisions within the boundary of the responsibility any employee is given, allows the employee to thrive in an environment of growth and fulfillment.

From the employee's perspective, the manager can be someone to tolerate, however the leader is someone they will be inspired to follow, look up to. Which would you rather be: Someone to be tolerated or someone to look up to? The keys that follow are ideas to help you be more of an inspiring leader than a tolerable manager.

> *"Leading with inspiration requires the leader to substitute authority with an empowering style of management that allows the people they lead to take control."*
>
> *−J. L. Ashmore, Author, Speaker, Consultant*

Walk Your Talk

> *"Setting an example is not the main means of influencing another, it is the only means."*
>
> *−Albert Einstein, Physicist, Nobel Prize Winner*

Think of times in your life when you have been told by someone in an authoritative position to do the opposite of what they themselves are demonstrating. The earliest image in my life that comes to my mind is my father standing in front of me as a teenager with a lit cigarette in his hand after he'd just taken a puff, saying, "I better never catch you smoking a cigarette!"

Most people tend to be more visual than auditory and therefore are more likely to do what they see than what they hear — as in monkey see monkey do. So, as a very visual person, I followed the example my father demonstrated physically before my eyes and tried smoking. It later became a habit. Fortunately, not too long after that I educated myself on the unhealthy aspects of that habit and quit.

So, as leaders, when we tell the people on our teams to do one thing, but they see us doing the opposite it promotes two things. First, it angers employees as we are inadvertently saying that the rules don't apply to us. It makes them feel less than — disempowered.

The second thing it promotes is the employee doing the very behavior we don't want them to do. It is again the monkey see, monkey do effect. Unconsciously, or maybe even consciously, the employee sees it as permission to follow in our footsteps. Or the employee demonstrates the undesired behavior out of a rebellious nature.

If you are an individual contributor in a company, not a manager, and striving to be an inspiring leader, how you walk your talk makes a difference as well. Do you think others on your team should speak up and communicate to management the thoughts and concerns your team has, or do you walk your talk and speak up yourself? Do you think management should solve all the problems, or do you see that shared responsibility and offer solutions to the problems? Take a look at where you can be the model and lead others by the example you provide.

The remaining ideas in this book are not of value unless you, as the leader, practice them yourself. The chapters have been written in a way to stimulate your own thinking of how you can demonstrate each of the keys.

> *"A leader leads by example,*
> *whether he intends to or not."*
>
> —*anonymous*

Take 100% Responsibility

> *"You must take personal responsibility. You*
> *cannot change the circumstances, the seasons, or*
> *the wind, but you can change yourself. That is*
> *something you have charge of..."*
>
> —*Jim Rohn, Author/Speaker*

When I was first exposed to the idea of taking 100% responsibility for my life, I didn't like it. This is true for many. Coming from the place of victimization can sometimes be easier, but it's definitely not empowering and not a practice that moves us forward. Once we are truly awakened to the concept, though, it's hard to put our head back in the sand and feel good about it.

Do we really have 100% responsibility for our lives? If that is a concept that is too much of a stretch for you or those you lead to grasp, let's try tweaking that idea and see if you find it more acceptable. Ask yourself, "What would be different if I were even 10% more responsible for my life?"

One of my mentors, Jack Canfield, the author of the *Chicken Soup for the Soul* series and *The Success Principles*™, taught me an equation that is powerful to follow and an example to demonstrate it. The equation is E + R = O. Spelled out, the letters stand for Event + Response = Outcome. This is a perspective even the most doubtful can relate to.

If we feel we have no power over a particular event (E), what we do have power over is our response (R) to that event. Jack's good example of this comes from the Northridge, California earthquake in 1994 where a news reporter was interviewing commuters stuck on the freeway trying to get to work the morning after the quake. You may have never been in an earthquake, but anyone who commutes to work in traffic every day will relate. One driver's negativity was apparent when he ranted about the stopped traffic, the time being wasted, and the inability of the authorities to impact the congestion. The next driver interviewed was smiling and saying how he was able to have his coffee and listen to the book on tape he had in his car; relaxing in the acceptance that he would get to work only as fast as the traffic would take him. One got to work stressed and angry, and the other relaxed and ready to work. Their response may not have impacted the timing of the outcome, however it definitely affected the outcome (O) — more relaxed and productive upon arrival — plus the fact that avoiding stress is a major component of maintaining health.

Most people will not be able to agree that they are 100% responsible for their life. It's certainly not common for one individual to see his or herself as contributing to a natural disaster. But what aspect of this principle can you use to improve your life and circumstances? Try asking the question, "What would change in my life if I were just 5% more responsible for my responses to the events in my life?"

What might be ways that you as a leader demonstrate the opposite of taking 100% responsibility for your life in general or specifically your life at work? What do employees or co-workers see in your actions and behavior that would inspire them to take on this belief or even 5-10% more of this belief?

> *"My philosophy is that not only are you responsible for your life, but doing the best at this moment puts you in the best place for the next moment."*
> —*Oprah Winfrey, Movie/TV Celebrity*

Do Away with the Complainers Club

*"Don't listen to those who weep and complain,
for their disease is contagious."*
—Og Mandino, Author

The practice of complaining is a habit. It goes hand in hand with the last key of taking responsibility for your life. It is a habit that colors every perspective, action and outcome in one's life. And, in a group, it is viral in nature. Like a viral infection in the body, it can drain the positive energy right out of the team.

The first key to changing any habit is to become aware that we have the habit. Sometimes our complaining is up-front and obvious, and sometimes it is more subtle and internal, but equally damaging. As managers and leaders, we model either positive or negative examples of this behavior, and as well, can help others in seeing their own habits and the impact on themselves and the people around them. The virus can be nipped in the bud with effective leadership.

Smokey the Bear

When Davy Tyburski, an executive in a medical technology company, had his first vice president role, he had a challenge to face right off the bat. He had been in his company for many years and was seen as a friend and sometimes a "therapist" to those in his department. He realized quickly as a V.P.

he didn't have time to hear all the complaints nor could he be a full-time problem solver. He had to implement change immediately and stop what felt like the "complainers club."

Davy implemented a new system for problem solving. If someone in his department came in his office taking 10 seconds to tell him a problem they had with no resolution in mind, the conversation ended at 11 seconds. To bring a problem to Davy, they had to also bring in 3 possible ideas of how to fix the problem. Davy said this system alone cut the complaints down by 50%.

He then implemented his "Smokey the Bear" system encouraging his team to find ways to prevent fires rather than being fire fighters. With this analogy and the constant reminders in meetings and conversations of being Smokey the Bear, another 25% of the complaints were gone. That was 75% of the complainers club gone with 2 creatively powerful policies.

There is a challenge you and your staff can take together. It is a challenge to stop complaining for 21 days. Any day that one person complains, the challenge starts over.

There is a website with support in doing this activity for yourself and with your group that can help you in the task. It is www.stopcomplaining.com.

When taking on this task, it is important to make some specific distinctions. In business, there are times when it is necessary to evaluate an event that has taken place and see what were the underlying actions, attitudes and behaviors involved in the event. We may do this whether our team has won the largest contract with a customer and we want to repeat that event, or it may be that we lost that contract and want to make sure we don't repeat it.

When an individual speaks of the reasons for an event turning out the way it did, there can be a reporting of the facts that is neutral. There may be a sense of the individual or team taking responsibility for the outcome or there may be a sense of them having been victimized by the incident. Talking about the reasons for the sake of evaluating is not a form of complaining or avoiding responsibility, but the attitudes when discussing the situation are what make the difference in a complaint or a report.

Also, there may be times when someone has an issue with a situation that is important for them to communicate to the manager or leader of the group. One practice some groups will put in place is to only allow these "complaints" to be voiced if there is a solution that is presented at the same time as the complaint. This encourages more responsibility and problem solving. At the same time, it addresses the concern some employees may have when they see their manager promote the "stop complaining" campaign that they think means they can never express a concern about something that they see needs to be changed. It's not intended to stifle communication, but to keep a sense of responsibility in the culture of the team.

For more information on ideas to stop complaining go to www.stopcomplaining.com.

> *"Ninety-nine percent of all failures come from people who have a habit of making excuses.*
> *—George Washington Carver, American Scientist*

Chapter 1: Aspire to Inspire

CHAPTER 2

V - Vision
of Purpose

Why do you get out of bed in the morning? What motivates and inspires you? These may seem like serious questions to ask in a business environment, but until someone can express a purpose to their life, they are wandering through life as a passenger on a bus rather than being the driver behind the wheel. Whether someone's purpose is related to their family, work, hobbies, creative outlets, religion, or wildest dreams, a lack of awareness around that purpose can create a mental fog and lack of clarity that keeps them mentally asleep.

Companies create a vision and purpose for being. Why wouldn't every individual do the same? Vision and purpose is the same as having a destination in mind when you leave on a driving trip. If you don't know where you are going, who knows where you will end up?

Even if your employees possess a purpose in life that is something other than the work they are doing for your organization, it is important for them to see how their job supports or is related to their purpose. Without that clarity, the employee is more likely to be resentful, unfulfilled and likely not engaged in their work.

Inspiring leaders work with their people to identify what the individual's life purpose is. The individual then can see how their current job supports that life purpose or will help lead them to manifest that vision. Another way to look at purpose is to focus employees specifically on the purpose or "why" of doing the job they are currently in now.

Is It Personal or Business

While Davy Tyburski, who I mentioned previously, is now known as Chief Profit Officer™. When he was with the global medical technology company, he was a memorable model of how to help people see (beyond getting a paycheck) their reason for getting up every morning and coming to work and for doing a good job. The medical technology that Davy's company developed and sold to hospitals helped patients recover from spinal cord injuries and severe burns as well as other conditions.

Davy guided employees to see their purpose in working for the medical technology company by asking them to look in their lives and remember family or friends who had suffered injuries that the company's technology could have helped. If they did not have someone they knew who had already suffered a serious injury, he had them think of who they would want to have access to this equipment if they were in an accident. He encouraged employees to put a picture of the person or people they identified by their desk as a reminder of why they do their job.

To model this for his team, Davy shared his own "why" story of a classmate of his that was killed in a vehicle accident. Davy's friend could have been helped or maybe even saved if he had access to his company's equipment in the emergency room. Making it personal is a powerful example of how to identify the reason/purpose for doing your job and doing it well.

Davy also supported individuals in uncovering their life purpose which may be the same as or broader and more personal than the service that was being provided by their job. On a personal level, Davy carried with him a picture of his family and on the back wrote the dollar value of the stock options he had with the company which served as a reminder for striving for that goal knowing that it would provide a valuable top-notch education for his two sons. Davy is an effective leader who inspires others by both walking his talk and helping others see their vision of purpose.

So, helping employees identify their purpose and tying it to their daily activities is an important part of helping them to do their best in their work. But, how do you do this?

First of all, it is important for the manager or leader in any group to be clear about his or her own unique purpose in life. It is part of our responsibility as leaders to model this key. Determine your purpose, if you don't already know it, and then share it with your employees. Or have it displayed in your office. It is a statement of clarity about who you are as a leader.

Second, help your employees to create a statement about their life's purpose. On the following page is a simple exercise you and your employees can do to develop your/their purpose. You can do this in a group meeting or with each person individually. A good time to do so is during an employee's annual review. Your assistance in facilitating the process and showing your own purpose will be an opportunity to walk your talk and be a valuable guide.

Remind your employees that their life purpose can change as their life changes. It is not something you necessarily discover once in your life and is then the same forever. That is true for some individuals, but for many, their purpose will change as they mature, marry, have children, lose loved ones, or accomplish significant life goals.

The exercise is well worth the time and the ongoing review to maintain and tweak one's purpose as life continues. If you've not already done so, find and share your life's purpose with those that report to you and then guide them to do the same.

> *"To be a leader, you have to make people want to follow you, and nobody wants to follow someone who doesn't know where he is going."*
>
> *—Joe Namath, American Football Champion*

Exercise

Craft Your Life Purpose

Step 1:

List two of your unique personal qualities, such as imaginative and passionate.

_____

_____

Step 2:

List one or two ways you enjoy expressing those qualities when you work or interact with others, such as to assist and to inspire.

_____

_____

Step 3:

Assume your ideal world — exactly as you'd like it now. What does this world look like? How are people interacting? What does it feel like? This is to be a present tense statement, describing a perfect world as you see and feel it. Remember a perfect world is a fun place as well. Example: in a perfect world people are free to express themselves in an environment of joy, camaraderie and love.

_____

_____

_____

_____

_____

_____

_____

_____

_____

_____

Step 4:

Combine the three prior steps of this exercise into a single statement. Example: My purpose is to use my imagination and passion to assist and inspire myself and others as we are all free to express our talents in joy, camaraderie and love.

_____

_____

_____

_____

_____

_____

_____

_____

"Don't ask what the world needs.
Ask what makes you come alive, and go do it.
Because what the world needs is people
who have come alive."

–Howard Thurman, American Author

CHAPTER 3

A - Aligning Goals

> *If you want to be happy, set a goal that commands your thoughts, liberates your energy, and inspires your hopes.*
>
> *–Andrew Carnegie, The Richest American in the early 1900's*

Why do so many people avoid setting goals? For many, the fear of not reaching the goal, of failing, is a greater deterrent than the possible fulfillment and feeling of accomplishment when the goal is attained. There are other beliefs as well, such as deserving the goal, fear of the hard work that it may take to achieve the goal, or not knowing up front how the goal might be achieved. We will talk about such limiting beliefs in a later chapter, but for now let's focus on goal setting as a tool.

There are 3 components to setting effective goals. One, is it a goal that is worth getting out of bed in the morning? Two, is the goal achievable? And, three, is the goal measurable, so that you know when you have achieved it?

Motivating: If a goal is not worth getting out of bed in the morning, that goal is either not stretching you enough to make it exciting or you just might need more goals. You can look at setting goals in the following areas of your life: career, financial, physical/health, relationship. So, make sure your goal is big enough and motivating enough to move you forward.

Achievable: The topic of achievability is a tricky one. You want to have a goal that will stretch you, but you also don't want it to be so outrageous that the likelihood of ever achieving it keeps you from taking the necessary actions. This is different for each individual, so sometimes it takes practice in setting goals that are motivating yet achievable.

Measurable: A goal is most effective when it is measurable in both time and space. In other words, how much do you want to attain and by when? You may want to "lose weight," but an effective goal is to "weigh 150 lbs by 8:00 p.m. December 31, 2013."

Losing weight is a desire or preference, but your goal is specific and measurable. Without clear, specific criteria for measurement, the subconscious mind cannot get engaged in the process.

Now, the real trick, once you have set your goals, is to keep them in the forefront of your mind. Writing the goals on paper with the detail of the measurements is critical. Think of it as a way to communicate to that part of your mind that will be searching for ways to help fulfill the order for that goal. Some like to place their goals near their desk where they will see them daily and some like to keep them in a goals book.

If you are really serious about achieving your goals, read them 3 times a day. When you first wake up in the morning and just before you go to sleep at night is a good time to implant them in your subconscious. One other time in the middle of your day is beneficial as well.

If you have others reporting to you, have them do the same. The top 3% of achievers are clear about their purpose and goals. Are you one of them?

Exercise

Aligning Goals (aligned with your purpose)

SPECIFIC OBJECTIVE (How much…By when?)
Career:
Financial:
Relationships:

Exercise Continued

Physical/Health:

Other (Personal Development/
Spirituality/Legacy):

**A goal is something you want which is measurable
in time and space. How much...by when?**

*"If you are bored with life, if you don't get up
every morning with a burning desire to do things—
you don't have enough goals."*
—Lou Holtz, NCAA Football Coach

CHAPTER 4

L - Listing Actions

> *The secret of getting ahead is getting started. The secret of getting started is breaking your complex, overwhelming tasks into small manageable tasks, and then starting on the first one.*
>
> **–Mark Twain, Author**

Earlier in my career, one of my teachers, Tony Robbins, informed me of the concept of "Chunking It Down." Because at that time I would often try to do too much at once and feel defeated, it was a valuable lesson for me. Some people have an intuitive sense for this process and for some of us we need to be shown.

The Bucking Bronco

One of my clients, Mark, is a Regional Sales Manager in an electronics distribution company in West Maryland. Mark received a call from another branch of the company asking if he would take on a young warehouse employee we'll call Bob. The manager who called saw Bob as unmanageable and said, "If you don't take him, I'm going to find a way to get rid of him." Mark admits that he, himself, was in the midst of a move to a new geographical location and needed someone immediately to help with the heavy lifting. Bob had been raised and currently lived on a farm, so Mark thought, "Perfect, Bob's likely used to slinging bales of hay. He might be just what I need." So, Mark took him on.

Mark learned pretty quickly that Bob was a bit of what Mark calls a bucking bronco. He had more energy than he knew what to do with and had his sites on some lofty goals, but in his unbridled enthusiasm sometimes rubbed people the wrong way. Bob quickly moved from the warehouse to an inside counter job selling electronics. He had a clear vision of what he wanted, but he didn't have the actions or stepping blocks of how to get there.

Mark was just what Bob needed to funnel his energy and enthusiasm into productive activities. Mark chunked down into daily doable actions what Bob needed to reach his goal of being number one on the list of all inside sales people. It also slowed Bob down a bit so he didn't rub people the wrong way. Bob began at 95th on the list; then moved up to 55th; then 23rd and finally number 1! Bob eventually moved to outside sales and is currently one of the top sales people in the company. What was seen as a throw-away employee in the beginning turned into a valued resource through one inspiring manager's patience, direction, and guidance in how to break down a goal into daily doable actions.

Tools for Taking Action

There are many valuable tools to help us "chunk down" a project or goal we have set. One way is within an outline format. Another is with a Mind Map. To create your own Mind Map, you can start with an 8 ½ X 11 piece of paper with a 2 inch circle drawn in the middle. Write the name of the project, such as writing a book, in the middle of the circle. Then draw lines out from the circle like a wheel. Add additional circles at the end of each line. In each of those circles, write the tasks that it will take to complete your project. For the writing of the book, they may be outline, research, publishing, cover design, editing, etc. Next to or within each of those circles, list the steps for each task. For cover design, they may be 1) network for referrals, 2) interview/select, 3) create/submit spec list, 4) edit proof, and 5) approve final copy. Highlight or check off each step and task as it is completed.

Another way to support your taking action is to create a list of 3-5 things each night to do the following day that will move you toward your goal. If you or your employee have a teammate or colleague that can hold each other accountable, those individuals can check in at the end of each day to report on what they have accomplished and the next day's actions they will commit to do. They can be called an accountability partner.

The founder of McDonald's, Ray Kroc, said, *"There are three keys to success: 1. Being at the right place at the right time; 2. Knowing you are there; and 3. Taking action."* I don't know who currently takes credit for the following, but a long time ago someone pointed out to me that the last word in *satisfaction* is a-c-t-i-o-n. So if you want more satisfaction, you've got to take more action.

So that you're walking your talk, take your list of goals from the last chapter and list on the next page 3 actions you can take in the next week towards that goal. Or if you really want to move forward more quickly, list 3-5 actions every day. Checking off and updating your list consistently will ensure you are continuing to move closer to your goal each day. What are you waiting for? Take action, NOW!!

> *"Vision without action is daydream. Action*
> *without vision is nightmare."*
> *—Japanese Proverb*

Exercise

Listing Actions

Listing Actions (by Goal)
Career Goal: Actions:
Financial Goal: Actions:
Relationship Goal: Actions:

Exercise Continued

Physical/Health Goal: Actions:
Personal Development/Spirituality/Legacy) Goal: Actions:

"Take the first step in faith. You don't have to see the whole staircase, just take the first step".

−Dr. Martin Luther King Jr.,
Minister/Nobel Peace Prize Winner

CHAPTER 5

U - Undo
Limiting Beliefs

Anything you can believe,
you can achieve.

–Napoleon Hill, Think and Grow Rich

Have you ever noticed the unfortunate function of the mind and situation that can occur in life whenever we set a goal? The mind will bring forth an image or life will present a situation either of which may appear as an obstacle to reaching our goal. Our response may be to kneel down and say, "Uncle!" to the obstacle or to find our way through or around what is in the way.

Many times the real obstacle we are facing is the limiting beliefs we have deep inside. They might be thoughts such as:

- "I'm not worthy of this goal."

- "I'm not capable of doing this.", or

- "I'm overwhelmed with what it will take
  to achieve this goal."

These limiting thoughts and beliefs often stem from our childhood or from experiences we have had or have seen others have as adults.

We all have the right to believe what we believe. A belief, after all, is just a thought that we attach to or that we are habitually thinking. However, some beliefs may hinder us on our path to success. As Sigmund Freud said, *"Thought is action in rehearsal."* When we change our thoughts, we are inevitably changing our actions.

Believing You Can

In the mid-nineties, Julianne Gardner took the position of District Sales Assistant for Paychex, Inc. Within 10 months, she could see an Outside Sales Rep was what she really wanted to be. At Paychex, it just wasn't an approved path to go from an assistant to outside sales, but with the support and belief in her from her District Manager, Mark Ealy, Julianne was promoted to Outside Sales.

That was the good part. The tough part was the territory she got had not generated revenue for 7 years! When the reality of that set in, she knew she would have to work harder than she had ever worked before to succeed. Julianne told her boss, Mark, that she would do whatever he told her to succeed. But after a time, she still was not seeing what she had hoped from her hard work. She had always had a positive attitude, but this was taking more than she could muster on her own so at the end of each day, she would go back to the office to get inspiration from Mark and share her activities, get feedback, and make sure she was on track.

Mark was the epitome of an inspiring manager for Julianne. He encouraged her with analogies that she was tilling the ground of her territory, moving rocks and boulders, planting the seeds, and watering. He gave her inspirational quotes from other leaders like Deepak Chopra and Brian Tracy, and affirmations she repeated daily to ward off any limiting beliefs that tried to arise in her mind. He recommended books, and at the same time supported her in the daily cold calls and other activities required for her job.

With the support and guidance of this inspiring leader, Julianne finished her first year, making her quota and going to St. Thomas for the company's sales incentive trip. With the continued support of her leader, she became the #1 sales rep out of 650 nationwide. Julianne later became a District Manager herself and with her took the model of being an inspiring manager that Mark Ealy had given her and passing it on to those she led. One of her employees,

Jill Caton, who had been with Paychex for over 18 years, told Julianne that she was the best manager she'd ever had. What a ripple effect an inspiring leader can have for waves of other employees and generations of leaders to come!

There are many books and methodologies on how to change a limiting belief. A couple of my favorites are *"the work"* by Byron Katie, and *"Tapping into Ultimate Success"* by Jack Canfield and Pamela Bruner. You can buy these books or search the Internet for more information on these specific processes.

Another simple process to clear a limiting belief follows.

Five Simple Steps to Changing Your Belief:
1. Identify your Limiting Belief that's in the way.
2. What's the supporting evidence you are focusing on that maintains that belief?
3. Create a new Empowering Belief that supports you in moving forward.
4. Look for new supporting evidence of the Empowering Belief to focus on.
5. Repeat.

Here's an example:
1. Limiting Belief: I'm terrible at math.
2. Supporting Evidence: I got bad grades in math in

high school. I don't like math. Division is hard for me. I made a mistake on my taxes.

3. More Empowering Belief: I'm getting better at math every day.

4. New Supporting Evidence: I can balance my checkbook. I can effectively use a calculator. I'm taking a nighttime class in math. I like to play and am good at Sudoku. I'm practicing math every day. My Dad was good at math, so I must have inherited at least one of his math genes!

5. Repeat: Look for new evidence each day to solidify the empowering belief.

Step number 4 can be challenging sometimes, because you are creating new pathways in your brain. If needed, ask friends, family or a co-worker to help you find new supporting evidence of our empowering belief that your mind might not let you see or acknowledge. Persistence is the key. So, don't let the old habitual thought patterns sway your determination to change for the better. Practice changing your unwanted limiting beliefs into more empowering beliefs using the exercise sheet on the next page.

"Whether you think you can or think you can't –
you're right."
–Henry Ford, Founder Ford Motor Company

Exercise

Undo Your Limiting Beliefs

Step 1:

Identify your Limiting Belief that's in the way.

_____

_____

_____

_____

_____

_____

_____

_____

_____

_____

Step 2:

What's the supporting evidence of your limiting belief that you are focusing on?

_____

_____

_____

_____

_____

_____

Step 3:

Create a new more Empowering Belief that supports you in moving forward.

_____

_____

_____

_____

Step 4:

What is the new Supporting Evidence of the empowering belief to focus on?

_____

_____

_____

_____

_____

_____

Step 5:

Repeat Step 4 until your new empowering belief is solid!!

> *"It's not what you are that holds you back;*
> *it's what you think you are not."*
> *–Denis Waitley, Motivational Speaker*

CHAPTER 6

E - Express Success

> *...People who describe culture and values and how people behave – I've heard people refer to it as 'the soft stuff' – they often underestimate its importance.*
>
> *–Carly Fiorina, Hewlett Packard CEO*

hy do so many managers resist or avoid the aspects of their job that has to do with the employee as a person rather than the employee as "collateral" or a resource? It's true they can be seen in that regard, but it tends to objectify the individual rather than see them as a human being, a person. The skills required of a leader to inspire others have been referred to as "soft skills". As former HP CEO Carly Fiorina stated, *"The soft stuff actually is the hard stuff."*

Most will agree that communications skills are important for a leader to be successful, but how many take the time to make sure their communication skills are sharp? Just like the athlete who goes to spring training every year and works to polish his or her athletic skills, the leader has the opportunity to determine which of their skills are in play or have been dropped out due to stress, busy schedules, or a perspective that warrants adjusting.

I see the practice of communication skills like any other practice whether it be doctors practicing medicine, lawyers practicing law, or that person practicing their sport. We practice it to learn the skill and then practice more to keep it polished and discover new ways of playing or performing whatever skill we practice. I've been teaching and practicing communication skills for decades. I still consider myself — and all of us — a work in progress when it comes to communicating!

Albert Mehrabian, a psychology professor at UCLA, tells us that every communication includes 3 components: Body Language, Voice Tone and Words. Each component influences the impact of the communication by a different percent. They are as follows:

- 55% Body Language
- 38% Voice Tone
- 7 %Words

It's quite amazing to add the first 2 together and see that

93% of the impact on each communication is other than words! Let's look at each category in more detail.

Body Language

Our facial expression — smiling and relaxed or tense and angry — and other body language, such as pointing the finger as you are saying the sentence, also adds to the impact on the communication of that one sentence. How do you feel when someone points or shakes their finger at you while they are talking to you? Some people say they feel like grabbing it or biting it. That just indicates how strongly the impact can be on the communication. How about standing with hands on hips?

Many psychologists have talked about crossed arms. Although this can be interpreted as resistant or angry, it is one that some people do as a way of relaxing their arms and has no meaning. The facial expression combined with the crossing of arms better defines if feelings of anger, judgment, or resistance are being communicated. It's important to take all three into consideration: body language, voice and words to determine the full spectrum of meaning in our or another person's communication.

Many are more aware of the body language others use than what they might use themself. How can you become more aware of what your own patterns of body language are? Like any practice of awareness, it happens by noticing as you speak, asking others for feedback, and watching others to raise your own awareness of patterns.

Voice Tone

There is more to our voice than just tone. It includes tempo, cadence, volume and inflection as well. You can easily demonstrate this by saying a sentence and placing the focus and inflection on a different word. Say the following sentence 3 times raising the emphasis of your voice tone on the word that is underlined:

- "*I* didn't say you stole the money."
- "I didn't say *you* stole the money."
- "I didn't say you *stole* the money."
- "I didn't say you stole the *money*."

There are so many different tones we can use when we communicate. Which of the tones listed below have you heard yourself use when communicating to your employees?

Angry	Loud	Uncaring
Caring	Nervous	Quiet/Calming
Condescending	Demeaning	Reprimanding
Demanding	Playful	Blaming
Elated	Loving	Judgmental
Humorous	Understanding	Compassionate
Joyful	Sad	Gentle
Kind	Apathetic	Harsh

How many times have you heard someone say: "It wasn't what you said, it was *how* you said it!" If that's being said to you and you find yourself resisting hearing it, there's most likely reason for you to take note. Voice inflection, cadence, volume, rhythm, pace, and style all have an impact in this category. It is important to be aware of how we deliver our communication.

We have control over our voice. If you are unaware of some of the tones or styles you may project, get a voice recorder and speak different ways into the recorder or use your voicemail recording to practice. Practice using tones that will *enhance* your communication resulting in more awareness of those that will *detract* from the effectiveness of your communication.

Words

The fact that "words" only have 7% of the impact on the communication doesn't mean that they are not important. The words you choose are also very, very important. It just shows how very influential body language and voice tone are on the impact of the communication. Of course, there are times when the choice of words can cut through the heart leaving the voice tone and body language in the dust!

So let's take a look at words and see some that commonly help or hurt your work relationship. How do you feel when someone says to you, "You *have* to...!" or "You *need to* ...!"

or "You *should/shouldn't*...!" Many times over the years in workshops, I have asked participants how they feel when they hear those phrases. About 75%-80% of people say things like it makes the hair stand up on the back of their necks and makes them feel like doing just the opposite.

Who in your life has told you most what you have to, need to, or should/shouldn't do? That's right...your parents or whoever held the parental role for you as you were growing up.

Below are some alternatives to what words are helpful and which are not so helpful in your communications with others. As you read them, think about which ones you might have habits of using.

Unhelpful Words/Phrases	Helpful Words/Phrases
You have to/need to/should	It's important/ valuable/ helpful/ the consequence of X is Y
Always/never	Sometimes/X number of times
Everyone/No one	This person/X number of people
I'll try	I will/ It is my intention
I can't/I won't	I'm unable/ I can do this much/ It's my choice or preference

Sometimes the words on the left may be accurate to use. However, notice when you use them, if using them is helping your communication be delivered and received in the best way possible. Or does it invite the other person to feel hurt, shut down, rebel, or turn away. In situations where you can use the words on the right, you may show more respect for others.

We can check in with those we lead and ask them what words they may find particularly negative or wonderfully positive. I have heard some people agree, "If you don't *should* on me, I won't *should* on you." Your choice to use or not use the phrases on the right above again shows a reflection of your respect for one another.

5 Times More Income

As Strategic Account Manager at a technology company, Aleesa Daley, had an office next to, Zack, the CEO of the company. Aleesa had established a relationship with Zack when she first started with the then small company and had been fortunate to maintain that relationship as the company grew for the inspiration that Zack brought to her.

The company was in rapid growth and as happens during those times, gaps will sometimes occur between the customer's expectation and what is delivered. Whether the gap comes from sales, service, or the product, the complaint from a large customer account about an unmet expectation comes back to the Strategic Account Manager, sometimes by way of the CEO.

Zack's skill was in delivering feedback in a way that kept Aleesa feeling positive about her job and her quality of work. He trusted her, consistently conveyed her importance to the company and backed her on decisions she made. What was great about Zack's style was his ability to use humor and keep a jovial tone even when the situation could have called for a more serious manner. He was deliberate in his choice of words, voice tone and body language.

Through Zack's support over the years, Aleesa increased the revenue she brought into the company three fold which increased her personal income by almost 5 times. Executives like Zack know that creating an inspiring environment through encouraging styles of communication and positive feedback allows individual contributors to flourish and the end result being better business all around.

> *"Communication is a skill that you can learn. It's like riding a bicycle or typing. If you're willing to work at it, you can rapidly improve the quality of every part of your life."*
> *—Brian Tracy, Author/Speaker*

CHAPTER 7

S - Strengthen
with Feedback

*Any fool can criticize, condemn,
and complain...and most fools do.*

**–Dale Carnegie, How to Win Friends
and Influence People**

When an employee hears a manager call them into the manager's office, the first thing that comes into most employees' minds is, "Uh oh, I'm in trouble now." There is a feeling that they are going to hear something negative.

Where does this automatic response come from? For many, it is a conditioning that came about in childhood from our parents. For even more, it is a conditioning that came about as an adult from our managers.

There are two kinds of feedback — affirming and constructive. Most people don't like receiving constructive feedback. Because of the use of ineffective body language, voice tone and words, constructive feedback often leaves people feeling shamed, belittled, less than, un-empowered and resentful. Both managers and employees see it as negative. It can be more destructive than constructive.

What if we look at feedback differently? Try taking the perspective that all feedback is positive. The root of the word constructive is "construct." The definition of construct is to build. When we start with the person and where they currently are and build on that when giving feedback rather than tearing down with destructive feedback, the person is much more likely to change their behavior.

Sea World

At Sea World in San Diego near where I live, trainers have a daunting task when faced with training a whale to jump over a rope 20 feet in the air. As leaders we face daunting tasks, but how many of us have faced training a whale? Well, O.K., sometimes our tasks may feel like we're trying to get a 10,000 pound whale like Shamu to jump!

The trainers at Sea World focus on reinforcement of positive behavior. They start with the rope under the water and give the whale fish, pats, play and lots of attention when it goes over the rope. If it goes under the rope do they punish the whale by reprimanding, stunning it with an electric shock, or giving threatening warnings? No, they ignore the negative behavior and only work to reinforce the positive behavior.

What can we learn from this as leaders? Studies show people need 3 times more affirming feedback than constructive feedback to function productively. How many managers give 3 times more affirming feedback in a week's time to each employee? In most cases, the opposite is true. Three times more constructive feedback is given than positive.

The 3 A's - Acknowledge/Appreciate/Assure

To inspire others, let's focus on 3 ways we can help to reverse the habit of only giving feedback when something goes wrong. Let's look at acknowledging, appreciating, and assuring.

There are many ways of acknowledging an individual. A "good morning" greeting is a way of acknowledging. Passing someone in the hallway and nodding is a way of acknowledging. Drop out one of these simple ways of acknowledging, and we have the opposite — discounting. There are many ways of acknowledging someone for a job well done.

If you're a manager, have you ever said, "Thank you for coming to work today." to an employee as they left at the end of the day? You may find a shocked look on their face, but once the shock wears off, a feeling of having been valued is left in its place. Simple gestures of thank you, appreciation, go a long way in the workplace — especially coming from a manager.

When employees are told that they are fulfilling the expectations of their job, they feel assured that their job is not going away. It's also especially helpful when someone is new on the job to assure them they are on the right track as they are learning. It inspires people to do more and be more effective at what they do when their work is affirmed in a positive way.

You may think that these are simple ideas and that everyone knows they should do them. Why, then, do they get dropped out too often or ignored all together? It is too common when we get busy and stressed with deadlines and schedules to cut short these small gestures. Cut them out though, and we risk leaving our teams in the dull, dry environment that leaves employees feeling empty, unimportant, and undervalued in their work.

Try keeping tabs on yourself for several weeks. Note when you make one of the quick, Ken Blanchard, *"One Minute Manager,"* kind of compliments, acknowledgements, or affirmations that the employee can feel positive about. Keep track of the times you give constructive feedback as well and see if you can follow the guideline of 3 times more affirming than constructive feedback. Whichever way you tend to lean, just know it's a habit and the first step to changing any habit is becoming aware that we have the habit. The second step is consciously choosing to break the negative habit, replacing it with a positive one.

Square Peg in a Round Hole

At one point in her career, Patti Siwa was the Director of Sales for United Natural Foods, the largest natural food distributor of produce and packaged foods, in the world. Patti inherited an Inside Sales Manager (we'll call Beth) who was having some challenges in her job. After a short time of working with Beth, Patti received complaints from both customers as well as Beth's direct reports. Beth could get the job done, but the way in which she conducted her business was seen as less than friendly and caring. Among other complaints, one from customers was feeling offended by Beth's abruptness giving them the indication their business was an inconvenience to her. Beth's direct reports felt no matter how hard they worked or how well they did, that nothing was ever perfect enough. They felt nothing quite met Beth's standards.

In a feedback session with Beth, Patti told her of the complaints she had received. Beth was hurt by the complaints and didn't understand why this was happening. Patti acknowledged and appreciated Beth for the things she did well. She assured her she was not thinking of firing her, but sincerely wanted to help her find what was the best approach to fixing what was not going well. She coached Beth to see that feedback isn't bad. Feedback can be held as positive when it gives us the opportunity to grow or sometimes lets us know when we are off the course of what's best for us on our path in life's journey.

Patti encouraged Beth to look at what Beth liked and didn't like about her position as the Inside Sales Manager and why she was in the job. What Beth shared was the background of her family and their expectations about what roles in a career were a sign of success. Although Beth was really unhappy with the stress of her job and the responsibility of managing her direct reports, she was holding on to it because of family expectations. Patti realized Beth was a square peg trying to make herself fit into a round hole.

It took Patti a few months of coaching Beth including having her look at her top skills and what she liked doing best. Beth was a fabulous analyst and organizer. She liked process and statistics and worked well with people individually when they did not report to her. Ultimately, Beth took a job in Purchasing as a contributor rather than a manager and within a month of her new position expressed that it was one of the best decisions she'd made in her life. Beth told Patti how grateful she was for inspiring her to look at herself and have the courage to make the changes that were in her best interests. Patti was a model of an inspiring leader who empowered Beth with effective feedback to help her see the vision of what she wanted for herself, how to move through the blocks, and take the actions for a more fulfilling career and life.

Using the 3 A's — Acknowledge, Appreciate, Assure — and focusing on keeping your constructive feedback positive, too, will go a long way to ensuring you are an inspiring manager.

> *"I have yet to find the man, however exalted his station, who did not do better work and put forth greater effort under a spirit of approval than under a spirit of criticism."*
> —*Charles Schwab, CEO Charles Schwab Corp.*

CHAPTER 8

How to Create an Inspiring Environment

> *Your office or work station should*
> *be an inspiring space where creativity and*
> *productivity is enhanced so you can shine*
> *in the boardroom in front of your*
> *boss and co-workers.*
>
> **– Laura Morris, Feng Shui Consultant, Toronto**

The 2 aspects of an inspiring environment we will discuss are the physical environment and the non-physical environment. Both are important in supporting the forward momentum we want in our workplace, our teams, and our companies.

Physical Environment

To start with the physical environment, think of the places you've worked or visited that had surroundings that made you feel comfortable yet motivated to work. What was hanging on the walls? What colors were used? Was there a sense of order and cleanliness? Was there a sense of nature brought indoors or was there more of a feeling contemporary simplicity?

You may have differing degrees of control of how much you can change the major aspects of your surroundings like structure, wall color, furniture or floor covering. But most people can arrange their space or add color and design to enhance the feeling that one has while working in their given workplace.

Creativity is the key to adding spaces that are inspiring for each or all of the workers in an office. You can hire a professional to consult you, such as an interior designer or a Feng Shui consultant. Feng Shui is a 2,000-year-old philosophy of the placement of objects and the flow of energy in a physical space that you might consider incorporating into your workplace. I love what Donald Trump says about Feng Shui. He said, *"I don't believe in Feng Shui, but I use it because it makes me money."* There are many resources on the Internet where you can learn more about Feng Shui.

If it's not in your budget to hire a professional, it can be a fun and valuable exercise for a leader and his/her team to brainstorm and choose how they can create an inspiring physical environment. There may be one area that is designated for inspiring quotes that has a new saying each week for workers to contemplate each day.

A manager of a shoe store created a ritual that every employee was expected to follow. Before going out onto the floor for their shift, they read the company mission, the quote for the day and then touched the company mission poster as they walked out. There is a team spirit and more positive energy in the group after putting this ritual into place and the team loves it.

In the Silicon Valley office of Facebook they have hung a big 4 X 4 foot sign that says "What would you do if you weren't afraid?" It's an inspiring quote to help people think both big and out of the box. Some teams feel that decorating the space for the seasons or holidays makes a fun and motivating environment as well.

I had one client who tied her team's strategy for improved customer service into a fun, memorable, and inspiring environment. Once they created the vision of service they wanted to provide, they wrote it on a large 4 X 6 foot piece of paper on the wall. Then, they had a commitment ceremony and had each customer service rep show their commitment to the vision by dipping their hand in washable paint, stamping their hand print on the poster, and signing their name below the print. It was an inspiring poster that remained on the wall as a reminder of the team's commitment to extraordinary service.

These are just a few examples. The ways you can establish an inspiring physical environment are unlimited since they are tied to creativity. It just takes the willingness to let go of how it's always been done before and being open to see new refreshing ideas.

> *"Creativity involves breaking out of established patterns in order to look at things in a different way."*
>
> *–Edward de Bono,*
> *Author of Six Thinking Hats*

Non-physical Environment

The non-physical environment is the environment we don't see, but is certainly felt by the senses. You know the feeling you get when you walk in a room and you can tell if two people have been arguing? There's an energy you pick up on. Sometimes people get uncomfortable when the word "energy" is used in a business environment. It scares some people because it's intangible. Some just plain don't believe in energy. Science, however, has proven at this point that everything is made up of energy. So why, if we can be open to experiencing it, shouldn't we increase our awareness of it and work with it positively?

If you manage a team of people and there is one person in the group who is very negative, it impacts the whole group. If you don't handle that situation, then you are not creating an inspiring non-physical environment. It can bring down the motivation of everyone on the team.

There is a great example of this in *Hidden Messages in Water*. The author, Dr. Musaro Emoto, did some amazing studies in schools in Japan to determine the energetic impact of negative versus positive attitudes and emotions on the crystalline structure of water. He placed jars of water at the door when students walked into the classroom. They spoke positively or negatively to specific jars, based on how they were labeled, as they walked in every day. He photographed the crystalline structure of the water after they sent the positive and negative messages. The photos of the water showed beautifully shaped structures, like perfect snowflakes, when sent positive messages and unbalanced deformed structures when sent negative messages.

Some would ask what does that have to do with people and inspiring work places? Well, people's bodies are made up of 70% water, so if those differing energies impacted the water in the jars, how could it not impact the people? One negative person on a team can bring down the whole team and it's the leader's responsibility to coach the person to changing their behavior or to find a more appropriate place for the negative person to work.

A New Twist on an Old Theme

I have seen more than one company choose to create a more inspiring activity during the winter holidays than the same old gift exchange that employees sometimes find boring. The team members can exchange names in a drawing and then come prepared to acknowledge that person at the holiday office party.

Each person starts their communication by saying to the other person, "The gift you give me is...", "What I appreciate about you is...", "Or what I've learned from you is..." I've experienced this type of exercise myself not just at holidays but at the completion of a long hard project or class. The kinds of comments I've heard or heard reports of people saying are such heartfelt things as:

- "I rest well knowing you are on the management team."

- "You give me the gift of your clear communication."

- "You listen to me."

- "I knew the moment I met you we would be great teammates."

- "What I've learned from you is your quality of patience."

My observation is that often no one wants to leave the party or the class when this is done. The spirit of heartfelt, simple, authentic truth is spoken that creates a connection among people that is priceless. When managers step out and do something creative in a business environment, that sets the stage for team members to continue acknowledging one another on into the future.

So, the non-physical environment is the atmosphere in any given work place. It is made up of the attitudes, considerate nature of all the individuals, and interest in the people and work that is at hand. The atmosphere in a group begins with what the manager/leader is modeling for the group.

Many ideas have been referenced in the stories in the previous chapters regarding how a leader interacts with those around her or him. They are wonderful examples of both physical and non-physical ways to create an inspiring environment. What do you do that leads to an inspiring environment and what do you want to stop doing that is not contributing to an inspiring environment?

*"If your actions inspire others to dream more,
learn more and become more, you are a leader."*
–John Quincy Adams, 6th U.S. President

CHAPTER 9

Where's Your Commitment?

> *Use power to help people. For we are given power not to advance our own purposes, nor to make a great show in the world, not a name. There is but one just use of power, and it is to serve people.*
>
> **–George Bush, US President**

Where's your personal commitment to being a more inspiring leader? Are you up to the task of placing more time and energy to that side of your job? Or will you choose the status quo and settle for what's average? Each step of our own expansion to being more than we have been up to now is just that, an expansion. It's growth — taking ourselves to the next level.

I love the analogy of the transformation of the caterpillar to the butterfly. The process of becoming more than we previously were always takes some degree of effort on our part and the willingness to move through what's uncomfortable in the process of transformation. Remember what Carly Fiorina said, *"The soft stuff is the hard stuff."*

You may find the ideas in this book as new to you or great reminders of what you want to do in your work teams and organizations. Bringing out the best in others is not a new concept, just one that can get lost in the focus on the bottom line. But having the best bottom line is dependent on the work of every individual in your organization. And the effectiveness and motivation of each person is directly related to how they are treated by the leaders. In my opinion, if you're not making time to bring out the best in yourself and in others, if you're not inspiring them through modeling and mentoring, then you are not a leader.

You are then doing the opposite of inspiring, motivating, modeling, developing, or encouraging.

You are creating a drag on the movement toward success in your group or organization.

You are then the manager or executive to be tolerated rather than one to be followed, respected, and admired. It takes away from the success rather than contributes to the wellbeing of all involved.

Whether you are a leader with the responsibility of people reporting to you or an individual contributor who aspires to demonstrate leadership qualities, your responsibility as a leader is to inspire others to do their best through modeling and mentoring. It's what leadership is all about. Stop placing 90% of your focus on the management aspects of your job and start inspiring your employees and others around you. You will likely experience more fulfillment in your work and in your life as you support others to live and work to their fullest potential.

Bringing Your Heart to Work

Visionary and thought leader Sharon Drew Morgen, author, speaker and consultant, shared an impactful story in Chicken Soup for the Soul at Work. She had contracted with a company to teach a new sales technology that combined trust, integrity and collaboration in supporting a prospect's buying decisions. The participants shared with Sharon that they liked the technology but didn't believe that the company would let them use the skills. They said the company didn't really care about people and treated the employees like sub-humans, used abusive selling tactics for prospects and only cared about the bottom line.

Later, Sharon observed the participants working in the telephone bank and watched while a senior vice-president came over to speak with one of the representatives. He interrupted the rep in the middle of a conversation. He then walked over to another person who was on a sales call and asked him why he had a personal photo on his desk, since none were allowed. At the desk where Sharon was sitting was a memo from the same man, telling people they had to wear suits the following day and they had to keep their suit jackets on in the morning because prospective clients would be coming through the office.

Sharon waited for the senior vice-president to return to his office and knocked on his door. She told him she had a problem to solve and asked for his help. She told him of her classes to teach the sales technology that supports trust and collaboration and the students fear to bring it back to their desks. He didn't understand as he said, "If it makes money, why should they be afraid?"

Sharon said the man seemed gentle although his actions didn't indicate that. She asked him, "Do you mind if I ask you a really personal question that may have nothing to do with anything?" He nodded with a smile of acceptance. She asked, "How do you function at work each day when you leave your heart at home?" He narrowed his eyes and asked what else she knew about him. She shared that she was confused and that he seemed like a gentle person, but put task before relationship. She told him she felt that somehow she felt he knew the difference.

He asked her to dinner and for the next 3 hours shared his experiences as an officer in Vietnam who had to do bad things to good people. He spent his life believing that his goodness could hurt people and decided years before not to let his heart get in the way of his job. He shared his pain and listened while Sharon shared a pain from her own life.

The next morning Sharon witnessed this man apologize to his entire team for being disrespectful to them, and offered to make whatever changes they needed, so that they would want to come in to work each day. He also wanted to learn the new technology and offer it to trust that being at work wouldn't be harmful and might even be fun. This story represents what can happen when one heart-based inspiring leader steps forward to make a difference and another leader reflects back the lessons learned and becomes a more human heart-based inspiring leader himself.

> *"There are two ways of spreading light.*
> *To be the candle, or the mirror that reflects it."*
> *—Edith Wharton, Pulitzer Prize Winning Novelist*

NOTES

_____

_____

_____

_____

_____

_____

_____

_____

_____

_____

_____

_____

_____

_____

_____

_____

_____

NOTES

_____

_____

_____

_____

_____

_____

_____

_____

_____

_____

_____

_____

_____

_____

_____

_____

NOTES

_____

_____

_____

_____

_____

_____

_____

_____

_____

_____

_____

_____

_____

_____

_____

NOTES

_____

_____

_____

_____

_____

_____

_____

_____

_____

_____

_____

_____

_____

_____

NOTES

_____

_____

_____

_____

_____

_____

_____

_____

_____

_____

_____

_____

_____

_____

NOTES
